Words from Within

Vic Watts

Presentation by *BookLeaf Publishing*

Web: www.bookleafpub.com

E-mail: info@bookleafpub.com

ISBN: 978-93-95890-55-7

First edition 2022

DEDICATION

Dedicated to my mom who is the strongest
person i know!

Memories

I thought of you today
for the first time in weeks.
You still linger at the
back of my mind like
a distant memory
that I cannot escape.
I cannot help but
think of you,
after all you were a
big part of my life
for oh so long.
I thought of you today
and I couldn't help
but feel the sadness
all over again for
the way that things
went downhill so quick.
You linger in the back
of my mind like a
sour note from a
broken down guitar.
Hearing your name whisper
inside my head is
like hearing a an
unfamiliar chord in a
song I know that

I should have recognized.
I no longer think
of how things used
to be, but instead
look forward to the
way that things are
meant to be now.
Your name no longer
lingers on the tip of
my tongue like a
sip of fine wine that
I have yet to shallow.
Now instead it lingers
only in the most distant
of my memories.

Darkness Revealing

Moonlight shining,
Darkness surrounding,
Lots of power in the night,
Stories told and
Memories mesmerizing
Stories told and
The dice is cast
Lost in the darkness…
Forgotten by the light
Overwhelmed by the
Way things need to be
Overpowered by the darkness
That she feels inside herself
Wishing and praying
For the light to come
Thinking it will
Never breakthrough
Lost in the darkness
That is slowly
Shallowing her soul
Forgotten and broken
Desperate to escape
Drawn to the
Darkness within….

Our Destiny

Our destiny is ours ...
I love you and I want you to know how much …
I hope that in the end it will be ours …..
I hope that one day we can recall all the
memories that we are making right now.
I want to share everything with you … I hope
you
know how much I want to be by your side.
You are my total … you are everything
I have always wanted.
My heart is yours and it has always been
like this since the that we met..
I hope you always know how much I
love you and how much I want you.

My Love for You

5

You are my whole life.
You don't know how
much I love you.
You're my World.
Your presence is all
that I need. Yes, if
you are with me then it
will be a happy day.
I never make any
promises that I can't
keep. My promise to
you is that I will
always be by your side.
I never want to
separate from you.
I fall in love more and more
with each passing day.
Now I promise that my
heart is yours. It will
always be so. I never
want to share my life
with anyone other
than you.
I know that our
circumstances are

a little difficult, but
while I can I will be
by your side.
I never want to be apart
from you. While the
days may change
my love for you
every day grows. You
are everything that I
need to be make happy.

Twisted and Lost

Twisted and lost, broken and battered.
Lost in his own head,
lost in the darkness,
broken inside myself
battered by life's decisions.
Twisted around until I am lost,
Losing himself to what is inside,
breaking apart the darkness taking over,
swallowing him whole.
Fighting to get out,

But losing to oneself
Not knowing how to deal with
All the stress that it has
Created and bought alive.
Twisted up with the darkness
Lost within it
Broken because he can't get out
Battered by his own decisions.
Having played his games for
So long they now come to him
Naturally and cause him pain.
If only he could see that
His ways need to change.
Instead he continues to be

As he is and hurts all around him.
Laying twisted in the fires that

He has started, and can't get out of,
Shattered till unrecognizable.
Little embers that just need to be
Dusted away and thrown out.

The Survivor

Tangled in the web of lies
Having to forget who she is
Even though she feels lost.
Suffering in silence,
Until there is nothing left.
Ready to give up
Very close to the edge
Initially lost, suspended in time
Very upset with how things are going
On the edge and ready to jump
Ready to call it quits at any moment.
Losing herself to the thoughts
Inside of her head.
Throwing away her thoughts,
Thinking about the new
Beginnings yet to come.

Spirit Shadows

Separating the spirits from the real
Never knowing what to expect
Sensing the joy that is left behind.
Shaping our lives around
The arguments and accidents
that have happened.
Separating the spirits of our lives
The happiness from the sadness
The good from the bad.
Letting the pain seep out and
Flow into the happiness.
Allowing the light into
The darkness that's hidden there.
Clearing out the dust and
Binging on the times that
The light shattered the darkness.
Spirits slipping in and out
Of the shadows of the heart
Lying crushed on the floor.
Disturbed only by the shadows
Of the spirits that pass
Through in rhythm to the
Music playing in the background.
Burning and withering
Destroyed be the spirits

That cause the darkness to
Rise and take over the light
That is left in the heart that
Has just been tossed aside
Like a piece of non-essential
Trash on the floor.

Dancing Shadows

Dancing in the shadows
stomping her feet to be heard
twisting in the wind
and burying the past.
Leaving behind the negative
and looking forward to
the things that are positive.
Dancing with the shadows
letting her hair flow
down her back and
getting lost in the darkness
that is surrounding them.
Dancing toward the shadows
giving away her heart
and losing her soul
to the one who
stands beside her.
Dancing for the shadows
allowing them to have her
whispering in the ear
of the one she has
lost herself for and
wondering what she'll do
when the morning comes.
Dancing away from the shadows

hoping for a new beginning
praying it will come.
Quickly wondering how to
regain the light within
her life and experience
things as they are

meant to be experienced.
Dancing just to be dancing
expecting nothing in return
getting less than she
has ever really given.
Experiencing what it is
like to be truly alone.
dancing-shadows

Oceans Apart

We may be separated by

different continents,

or by the oceans themselves,

but that has not stopped the

love that we share.

The ocean is just water

it does not break the
emotions that we share.
The space of oceans
may pull us apart,
but our hearts are what
brings us together
in the deepest way possible.
Through the problems
we may face we stand together
against all the odds that
are thrown at us
together is where we still stand.
Across the oceans

a love has flourished
and together we will
fight to hold on to it.
The ocean may separate
but our minds and hearts
bring us together in a
way that only we understand.
So when we are feeling
alone we need only remember
that somewhere across the
ocean is the other
half of our whole heart.
We may be separated by
different continents,
or by the oceans themselves,
but that has not stopped the
love that we share.
The ocean is just water
it does not break the
emotions that we share.
The space of oceans

may pull us apart,
but our hearts are what
brings us together
in the deepest way possible.
Through the problems
we may face we stand together
against all the odds that

are thrown at us
together is where we still stand.
Across the oceans
a love has flourished
and together we will
fight to hold on to it.
The ocean may separate
but our minds and hearts
bring us together in a
way that only we understand.
So when we are feeling
alone we need only remember
that somewhere across the
ocean is the other
half of our whole heart.

Love Renewed

Stars burning,
fire emerging,
moon brightly shining.
The wind in our faces,
the sand beneath our feet.
Stars burning,
the fire ever emerging,
learning to balance.
relearning who they
are as a couple.
Realities changing,
lives finally blending,
Ending one story,
to begin another,
two parts of the same
story just written on
different pages.
Stars shining,
fires burning,
as they recommit
and promise to love,
unconditionally.
As they promise,
that their story has
not yet reached its end.

Letting their feet guide
them as their hearts
bring them back to
the story that is meant
to be their own.

Wishing, Hoping, Praying

Wishing things were different,
hoping for new beginnings,
praying for it all to make sense.
Wishing we still understood each other
hoping for patience
praying to understand the why.
Wishing things could go back
hoping to get the option
praying for forgiveness.
Wishing to be able to let go
hoping against hope for an end
praying for silence.
Wishing things could be changed
hoping to know how
praying for the same feelings.
Wishing things could have been different
hoping for the changes
praying for things to remain the same.
Wishing the differences didn't matter
hoping for the energy to suffice
praying to turn back the clock.
Wishing for the beginning
hoping for the middle and
praying for an ending.

Doubting Pain

Doubting herself,
thinking she needs to
find the beginning again.
Doubled over to think
not wanting to show
the tears that are
reflecting in her eyes.
Losing herself to the
agony that she feels
inside of her soul.
Pained by the loss
of what was most
dear to her heart.
Destroying herself to
make the pain go away.
Tossing away what once
was the most important
part of her life in
return for the happiness
that she so needs to
have around her.
Not knowing how to
react to all of the
loneliness and sadness
that she is feeling

deep within her soul.
Wanting to know that
everything will be okay
in the end, but knowing
deep down that it
will never be okay again.
Overridden by the loneliness
drowning in the pain
suffocating from the loss
that is yet to come.
Hoping she can bear
the pain and still stand
tall in the end of it all.

Dancing in the Waves

Dancing in the dark,
watching as their bodies
move slowly in the
waves that are crashing
against the beach.
Their ideas blending but
not quite meshing together.
Needing the closeness that
they share, but avoiding
the ultimate intimacy
of the uniting completely.
Feeling the passion of
their union without ever
touching each other.
Their connection so deep
that the waves become
just a feeling that is
washing over their feet.
Dancing though the waves
finding a balance that
is truly all their own.
Dancing through the waves
and becoming one with
each other without ever
having to touch.

Broken

Broken,
haunted....pained,
so many thoughts
whirling around in her head.
Tortured,
unsettled....withdrawn,
so many emotions
that cannot be explained.
Confused,
terrified…lost
stumbling along with
her head spinning
out of control.
Pointless,
prayers....unforgiving
doubts swirling in
her heart and in
her head and
destroying who she is.
What shall she do
to come back from
all of the pain
that she is feeling inside
right this moment?
Thoughts,

tumbling…tangled
all thrown together
making a mess in
her head that she
cannot understand.

Confusing Emotions

Loving you has come naturally,
losing you will tear me apart.
Not knowing what the future
holds has me mesmerized.
Tossing aside all thought
of anything that has happened.
Knowing that none of it
can be changed or redone.
I have found what I want
but of course it's impossible
to have because of where
things stand right now.
Looking into the eternal
glass I know that I am
not alone in any of this.
Sure you are not here
and never can be
but I know what that I
am not alone thanks
to how you treat me.
Torturing myself with the
same thoughts, things I
cannot seem to get out
of my head at all.
Losing myself in the pain

and emotions that I
have tried to keep buried
deep within myself.
Emotions that I should
not feel or even think

about because of how
things are right now.
Emotions that have to
stay buried because I
am too vulnerable to
fix them right now.
Things that I should
not be feeling no
matter how much sense
it may make to me.

Looking In Your eyes

Looking into your eyes
I see all of the emotions
that are reflected there.
I see the love and the
pain that is hidden in
the shadows of the
your past and burdening
your present because
you cannot let it go.
Looking in your eyes
I see everything that
you would rather keep
hidden, all of the hope
and love that you
wish to share, but
hide away instead.
Looking into your eyes
I see the devastation
that you know you
cannot cause so instead
you stay silent so
as not to hurt
the one you care
about the most.
Having the hearts of

two in the palm of
your hand and not
knowing what to do
with them, so instead
you try to shelter
them both so as
not to hurt them.
Placing them both
in your pocket and
hiding them both
from the pain of
knowing what is
and what will never be.
Knowing that it is
not something that
will be faced easily.
Looking into your eyes
I see all the emotions
that should be, but
shall never happen.

Buried Thoughts

Buried deep within themselves
is the emotions that they
have tried to hide.
The thoughts that are
raging to be let out
but instead shall stay
buried within themselves.
Never knowing what may
come their way in
the near future, but
instead playing along
with the fates and
ignoring the obvious.
Telling themselves that
what is buried shall
never come to the
surface at any cost.
Knowing that the thoughts
are things that will
have to stay buried
within the depths of
the nothingness in
their heads and hearts.
Solitude is evitable
because anything more
is not even a possibility.

Tip of an Iceberg

Sitting on the tip of
an Iceberg, sitting on
the brink and ready
to dive into the future.
Guess I really should
have known that nothing
was for real, that everything
sooner or later comes to
an end or becomes the future.
No one tells the truth
anymore, everyone lies to
move forward. I don't know
why it comes so easy.
On the brink of giving up
throwing in the towel
and ready to let it all go.
Broken for the final
time and sealing away
all of her emotions.
Done caring, done feeling!
On the tip of the iceberg
done with everything.

Empty Words and Broken Promises

Empty words and broken promises
that is all that is left of the
friendship you swore would never end.
This empty feeling deep within
inside of my chest if the heart
that you have once again crushed
because I believed in you.

Chills of sorrow is what washes
over me every time I think of
you any more, because you
have once again let me down
just like I knew you always would.

Fighting back the tears and choking
down the breaths that I struggle to
hide from everyone around me.

Destroyed by yet another of your
betrayals and broken by words
i thought you were saying
because you actually meant them.

Silly me for believing,

silly me for trusting,
that was stupid on my part.

I really should have known better
I really should have seen this
before now....should have recognized
that you were a liar all along.

Buried deep within my soul
is all of the empty promises
that you made to me that
you swore you would never
break.... silly me for believing
that what you said was true.

Standing on the edge of the
cliff looking down...and
contemplating just jumping
off into the emptiness that
has now taken over mysoul.

Debating whether it is worth
the pain to keep moving forward
with so many empty words
and broken promises spewing
from your lips and burning my ears.

Its now or never, I can't be
saved. Have given up and

jumped to late for me, but
perhaps one day you
will see that what was
should have been held
onto instead of thrown away
like trash....too bed it will be
to late by then to fix the
soul that has shattered.

Guess I Should Have Known

Guess I really should have
known that you would be
like all the rest.
That all the pretty words
were really just that.
Just pretty words to pass
the time until you felt that
you didn't need me anymore.

Guess I really should have
known that you would
walk away just the way
that all of the others
have done to me.

Guess I really should have
known that when you said
I was your best friend
you really didn't mean it.

Now i'm heartbroken just
as I have been before.
Wondering why people think
that they need to lie so
much and play with others

feelings to benefit themselves.

Guess I really should have
known that in the end you
would let me down again.

Everyone has, I just never
thought that you would be
the one to hurt me the most.
I never imagined that you
would let me down again.

Guess I really should have
known that our time would
come to an end that I'd be
the one to suffer for all
the kindness that I showed.

True friends listen to each
other. True friends do not
just walk away the minute
something doesn't go as
planned, instead they stick
it out and work together
to make each others lives
so much easier.

Guess I should have known
that in the end I was not

really your friend or anyone
to you really, because if I
was you would have not
been able to walk away as
easy as you did.

You would not have broken
my heart yet again. Guess
what they say is true
friends do come and go,
but I really thought that
you were more than that.
I really thought your words
were real and the things you
said were true. Guess I've
learned now not to open
myself up like that.

Thanks for teaching me
that trusting people,
that trusting a friend is
not something that I should
ever do again.

Broken Angel Wings

CREATIVE WRITING
POETRY
PERSONAL ESSAYS
MEMOIRS & BIOGRAPHIES
RELIGIOUS STUDIES
Broken Angel Wings
EMILYSEP 5, 2020
5 COMMENTS
broken-angel-wings
The wings may be broken

but the angel still flies.

Soaring high into the skies.

Looking and seeing everything

that is around her.

The wings maybe damaged

but even then the angel

soars finding comfort

amongst the clouds and

those who care for her.

The wings maybe tethered

but even with them shattered
the wind still catches.
Soaring higher into the skies.
Then making the descent
down the stairway of life.
Finding herself, exploring
what's around her.
Discovering that even with
broken wings she can still
soar as high as she wishes.
Discovering that even though
her wings are tethered she
still can hold her head up high.
Even with her broken wings
she soars high above the
clouds, higher still then even
she knew that she could
go to get lost amongst a
world where she can
feel secure and safe without
all of the pain that is
cast inside of her head.
The wings of the angel

may be tethered and torn
but her heart is now
free and her head is
now clearer than it
has ever been before.
The wings may be battered
but the soul is shiny and bright.
Having descended the steps
leading to the higher place
a place of surrender and
a place of peace within
her broken soul.
The wings may be shattered
but the Angel still stands
just as tall as if her wings
had never broken.